Hello I am Bumi who travel to learn
Come along on our journey and learn
Travel with my best friend Atlas and the amazing buzzing bee.
We will learn of income, business terms, and even world currency.
I love to dance and play
and I also love to share,
This will be the perfect day to show everyone how much i care.

Index

Introduction	1
Index	2
A: Asset	3
B: Bank	4
C: Compounding	5
D: Deed	6
E: Entrepreneur	7
F: Fiat Money	8
G: Grant	9
H: Hard Inquiry	10
I: Investment	11
J: Jackpot	12
K: Keogh Plan	13
L: Leadership	14
M: Money	15
N: Notary	16
O: Occupation	17
P: Passive Income	18
Q: Quid Pro Quo	19
R: Real Estate	20
S: Safe Deposit Box	21
T: Trade	22
U: Umbrella Insurance Policy	23
V: Value	24
W: Will	25
X: Xenocurrency	26
Y: Yard	27
Z: Zoning	28
Song	29

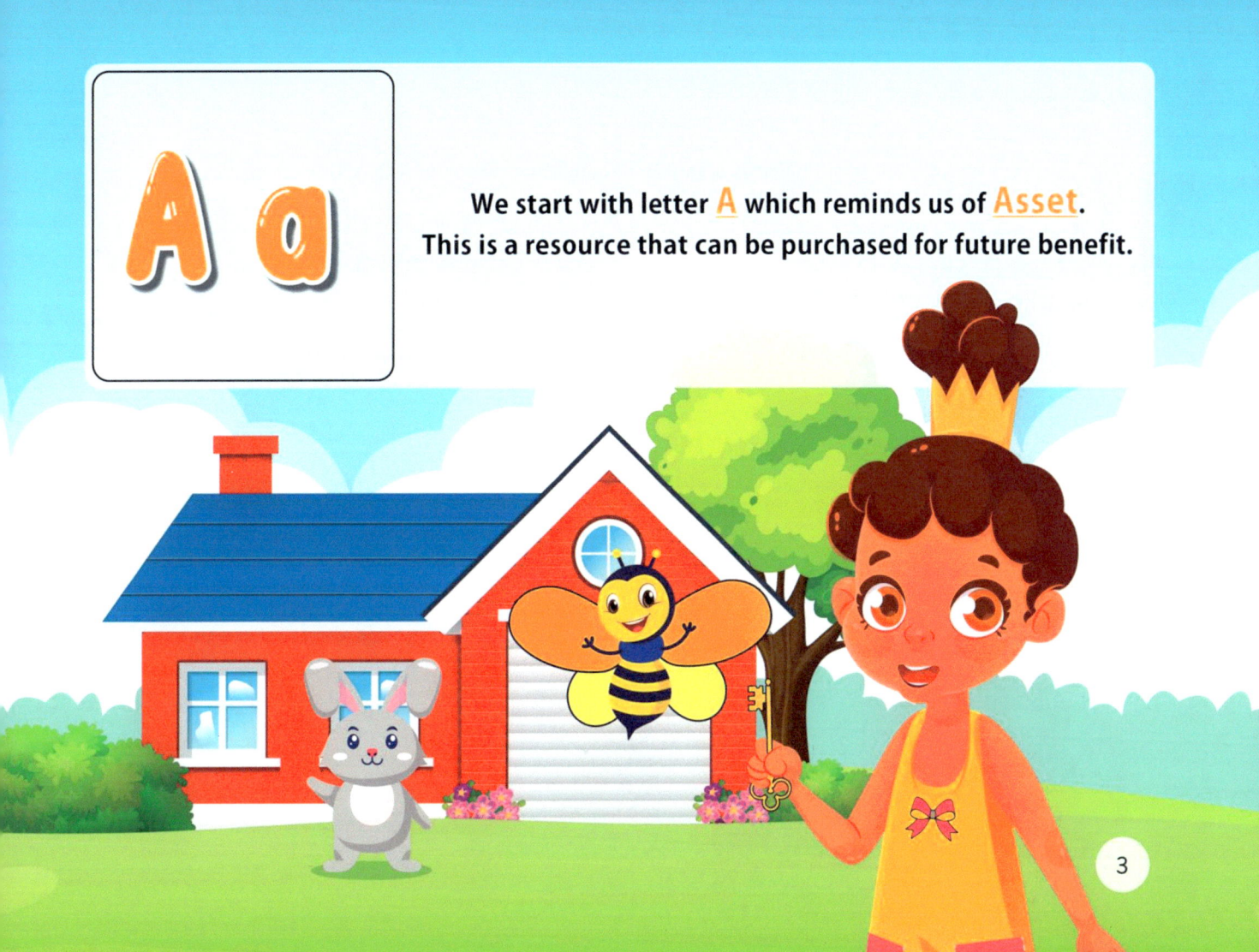

Then we buzz to letter **B** and we landed at the **Bank**. A financial institution where we deposit our money, oh i'd like to thank.

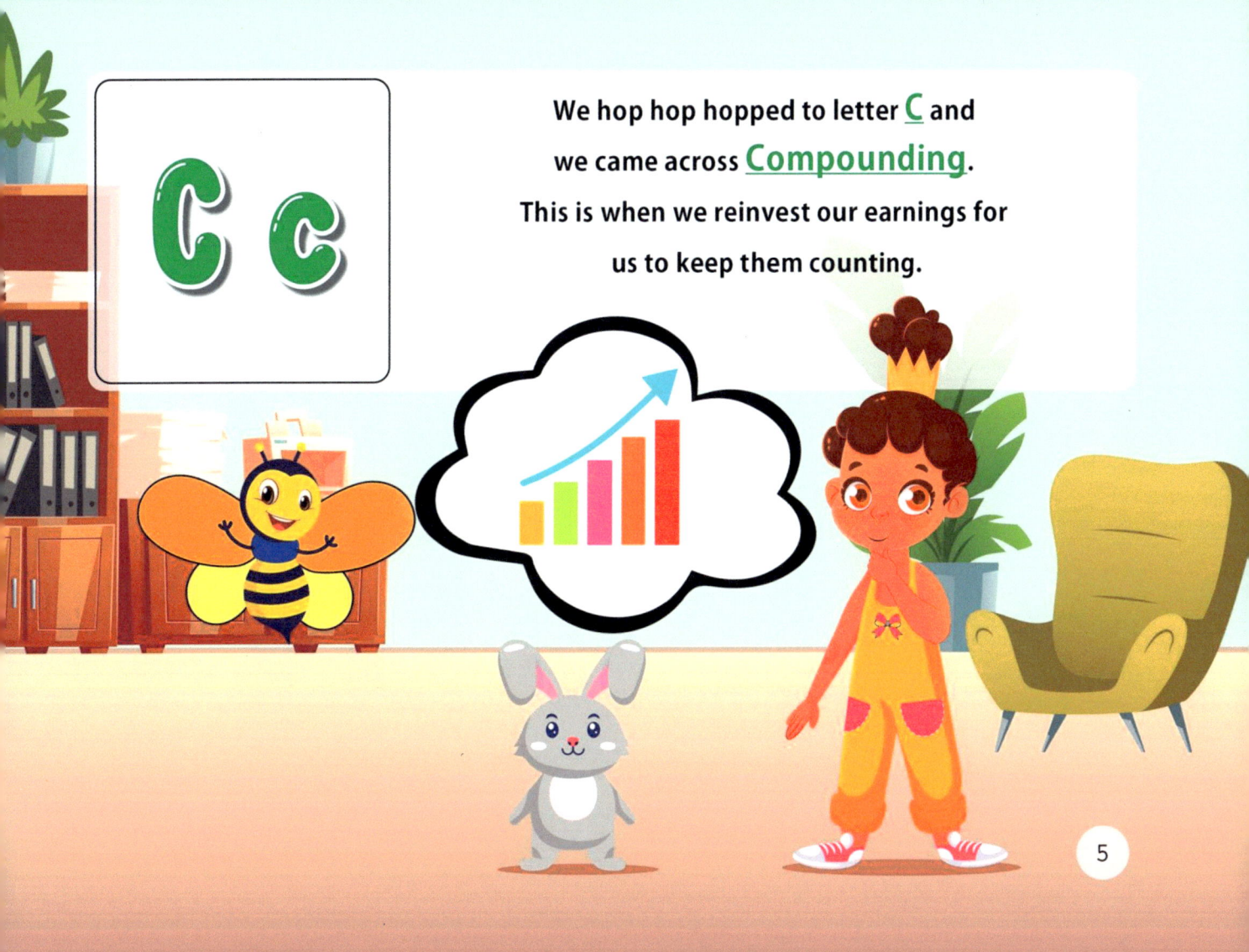

D d

Bumi saw the letter **D** and we learned about a **Deed**. A deed is a signed document that prove our ownership of property.

Travel with us to letter E as we prepare to be an Entrepreneur. Entrepreneurs use their ideas to start and operate a business, oh a journey to endure.

7

F f

The wind blew in the letter F and in Fiat money flew. Paper currency whose value is determined by the government who issued it to you.

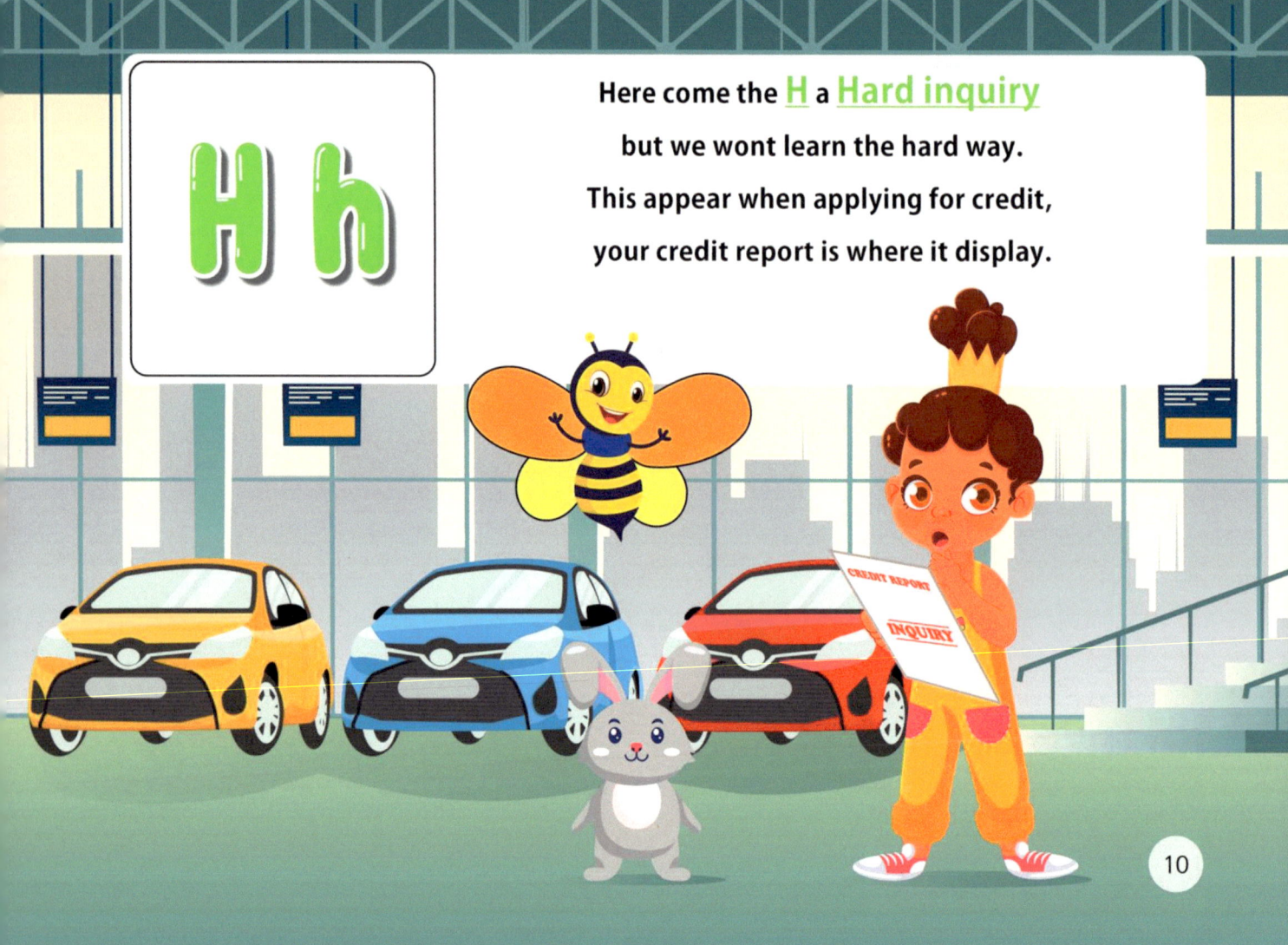

This one is exciting I teach us power of **Investments**.
Investment is like an asset we hope to double or triple the benefits.

J j

We jumped jumped jumped to J and then said Jackpot. Jackpot is getting large money in a short time, oh how lucky we have got.

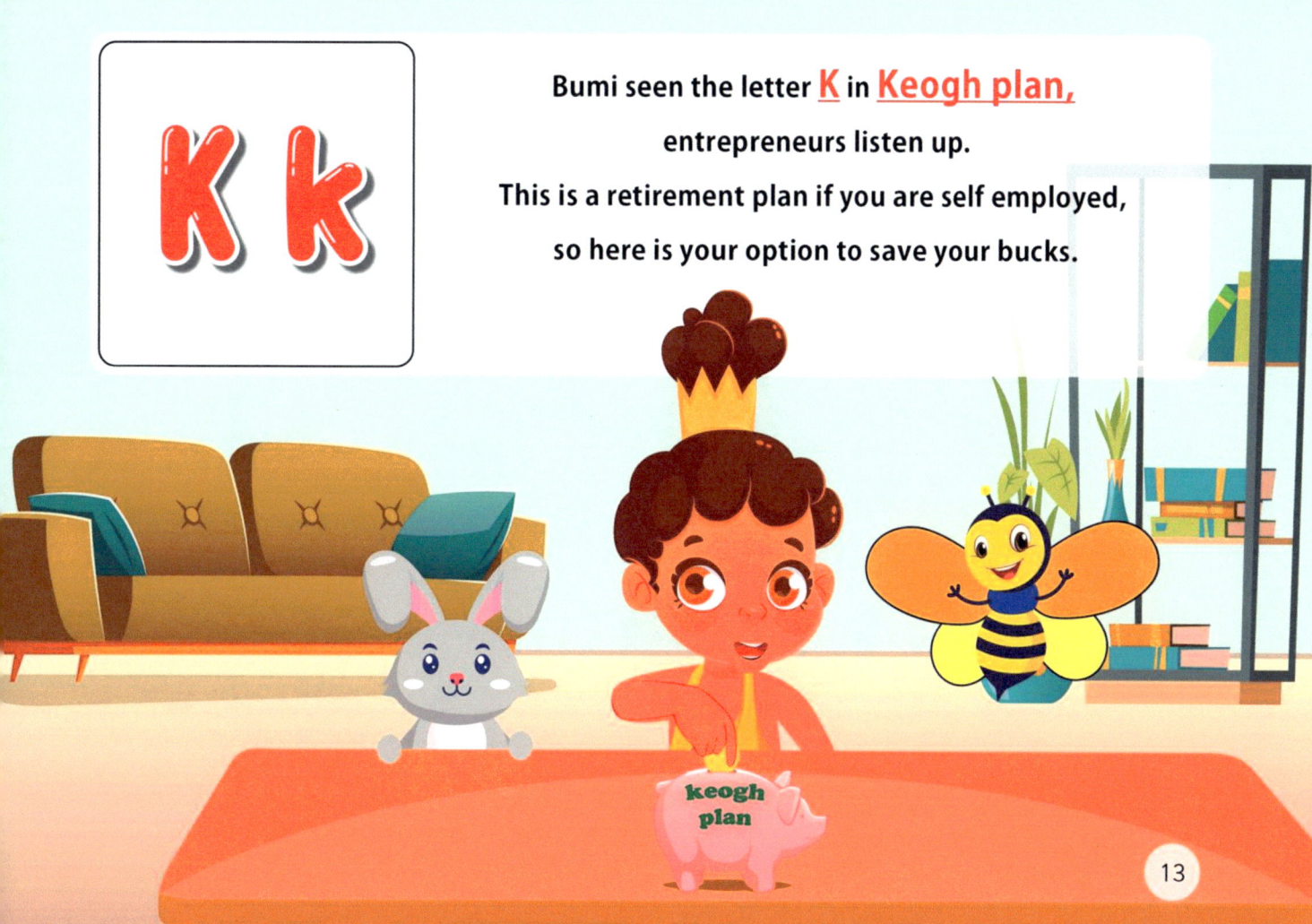

K k

Bumi seen the letter **K** in **Keogh plan,**
entrepreneurs listen up.
This is a retirement plan if you are self employed,
so here is your option to save your bucks.

The L was very strong because it taught us Leadership. With Skills of strength, courage, and knowledge leaders can offer tutorship.

I heard of the **M** it showed us what is **Money**.
A tool exchange for service and
goods, learning this was sweet as honey.

15

N n

Now we wiggle to the N lets learn of Notary. A public commissioned official who witness document signing, proving it is true to be.

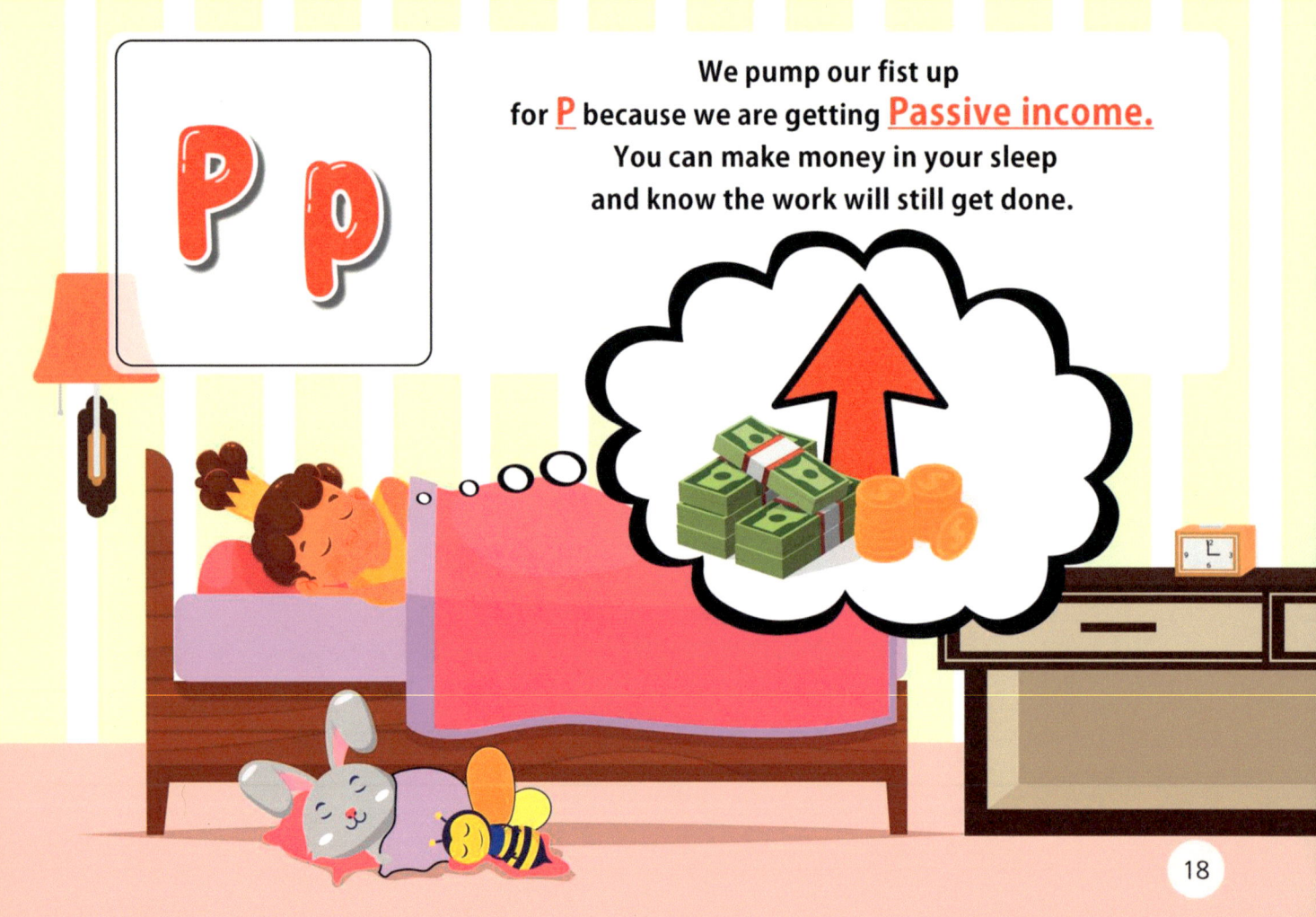

R r

Run run run into R and we landed on Real Estate. This is property of land consisting of resources or buildings , we can invest in this and make it great.

Come skip with us to **S** to learn of a **Safe Deposit Box**. We can store valuables at a bank or credit union to secure what we got.

We must all remember W it is the importance of a Will. These are documents of inheritance transferred when you're no longer here.

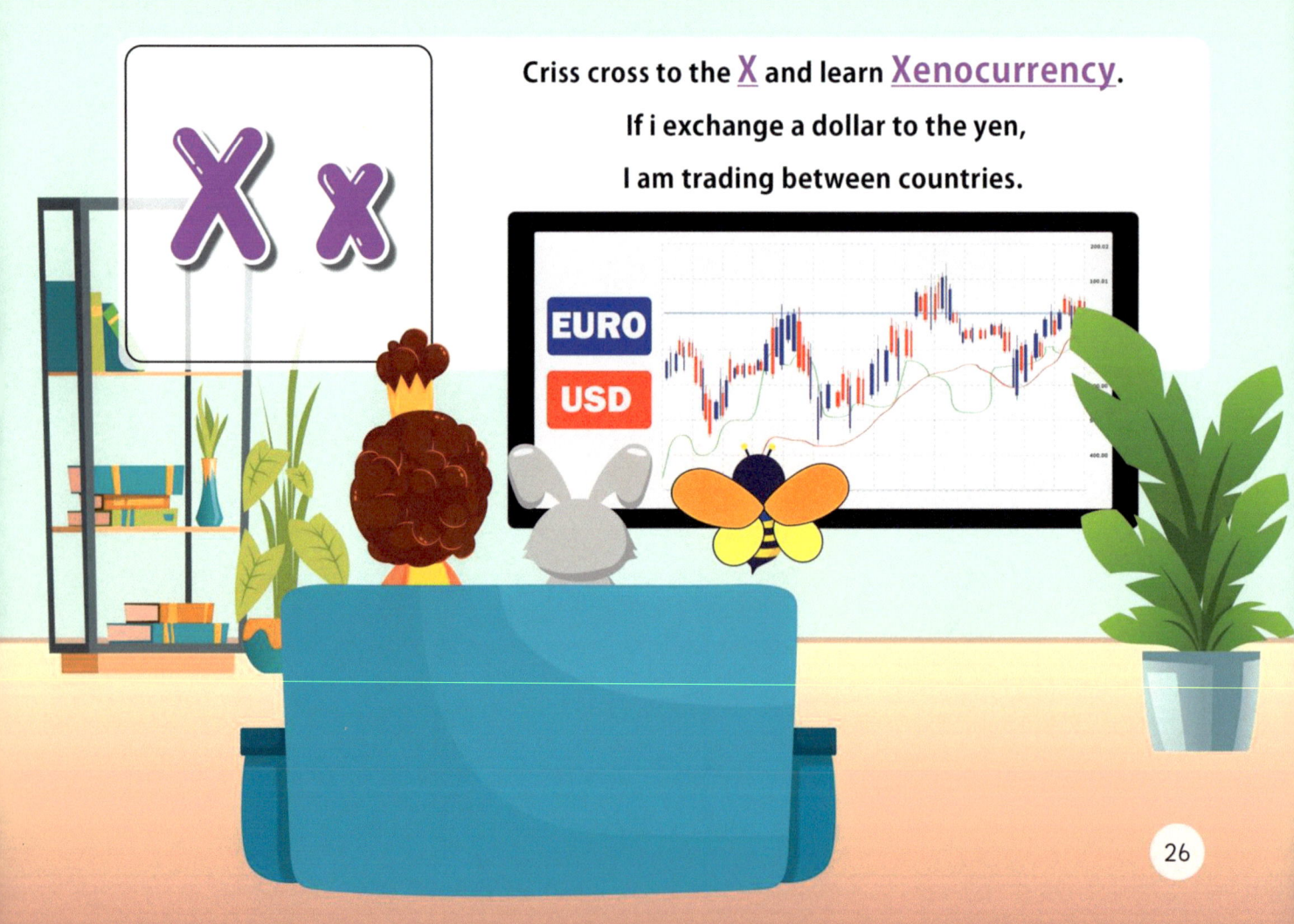

Don't sleep we are here at <u>Z</u> so we learn the laws of <u>Zoning</u>. This determine how buildings and land can be used within a certain area, and we can know correct owning.

We had fun learning terms
Now Sing it with me,

Now i know my ABC's ,
(Now i know my ABC's)

of financial literacy.
(of financial literacy.)

Learning these terms is such a delight,
(Learning these terms is such a delight)

I will be amazing and bright.
(I will be amazing and bright.)

Made in the USA
Columbia, SC
09 March 2024

32592144R00018